an unswept path

(a collection of monastery haiku – part one)

Malintha Perera

Copyright © 2015 by Malintha Perera

All rights reserved.

ISBN 978-955-42002-1-0

Malintha Perera
Colombo, Sri Lanka

email : malintha22@gmail.com

website : https://buddhistpoetry.wordpress.com/

Preface

This is my lens on the world after I began writing haiku. The space speak so much more than the words I've written. Please go slow, take your time and leave no gaps between the poem and yourself. Welcome to my monastery.

My deep gratitude to Mr. Alan Summers for encouraging me to present it to you. For his patience and guidance throughout my journey from the beginning. My heartiest thanks to Mr. Willie Bongcaron for opening the doors of Haiku Nook and for his guidance and love... for discovering me. I also want to thank Mr. Gabri Rigotti for his support he gave me from the beginning which I cannot ever forget. My thanks to all those at the Haiku Nook for their feedback and love that helped me to come so far. Thank you all my g plus friends and those in my Buddhist Poetry community for inspiration and much love and blessings. Thank you my family and my parents, my spiritual teachers... much love. May all be happy and free from suffering !

With Metta

Malintha Perera
September 22, 2015

Other books by Malintha Perera
Mind Your Own Business (a free book)
Kadupul (a free e book at smashwords)
download https://buddhistpoetry.wordpress.com/

Foreword

Gentle luminosity is an art not made easy when haiku writing can slide and veer into other genres such as aphorisms and epithets. Malintha Perera avoids the cliché and falling into the aforementioned traps bringing us to a world that is much needed.

Haiku are a mixture of little pockets of silence which are then popped by a nurse's needle so that they implode in our minds with a private firework display.

The best fireworks are not the expensive and explosive displays but the quieter workings in a night sky.

I have witnessed the growing of Perera's haiku writing skills, and where the scaffolding falls away to present a sunlit residence. Each window alternatively reflecting light from the sun, and also glimpses of the rooms inside. This is her residence, with an open invitation.

Alan Summers
Japan Times award-winning writer, Pushcart Prize nominated poet, and founder of With Words.

Dedicated to my family
    Duminda, Dinuga and Vinuka

monastery...
an unswept
path

early hours...
monks chanting
to a sleeping Buddha

warming up
with the moon...
a pond frog

mist
    overtaking
mist...
there's more to life

in stillness
I forget
to move

early spring...
the mosquito
with a broken beat

full moon...
the size
of my yawn

weaving breaths
one by one ...
I burrow
        myself

alms round...
a monk hiding
his begging bowl

a hanging edge
marks the white sand...
saffron robe

sound
of sweeping leaves
rising and rising

still pond...
the frog coming
out of a full moon

the sky
peeping through
a puddle

forgetting
the lines...
a tree frog

is that
a new song
mosquito ?

birthday sermon....
the monk tells me
there's no I

temple bell ...
I open my eyes and search
for names

full moon...
the candles become
one

insects...
I bounce between
their sounds

water
on the moon
comes
      and goes

the rhythm
of silence...
fireflies

forest rain...
the sound and I
become one

silence...
how the leaves
touch down

full moon...
the forest breathes
in and out

garden lantern... a firefly swallows a drifting flame

spilling moon...
the Buddha
is whiter

slow breathing...the forms take shape

full moon ...
a mosquito runs
out of breath

temple pond...
a frog says
too much

moonlight. ...
the jasmine
  is silent

A tensaku dedicated to Francis Franklin

temple bell....
the incense
b r e a t h e s

a big leaf
falling ...
   stem
down

abandoned...
   I breathe without knowing

moon flower...
each thought
is a dream

stone seat...
the mist bends
at its feet

dandelion fluff...
another search
for a self

deseeding

his own fruits. ..

a novice monk

swallowed
by sand...
a Bo leaf

patterning
the sand...
zen monk

Buddha posture...
I look around for the one
who coughed

darkness...
I search for a light
outside

evening prayers...
another mosquito
with a long drill

shrine room...
a shallow vessel
at Buddha's feet

meditation...

awakening to my

snores

the night sky

has taken a bite

out of the full moon

hitchhiking

in the full moon, another

wet leech

replacing

a leaf...

butterfly

bodhi tree...
here and there are puddles
of wax

there is no
going back...
cherry blossoms

stillness...
the sound of rain
that never came

temple bell...
monks turn
to face the wall

muddy road...

I postpone

to be by myself

A tensaku dedicated to Alan Summers

cupping
this moment...
a monk's moon

Plum Blossoms ; A HAIKU SERIES

words
gone for now...
plum blossoms

hanging
our thoughts
on the petals

our fingers
whisper
in buds

eyes linger
on the leaves...
tremble

they are us
but are we
them ?

these flowers
touching us...
touching us

www.ingramcontent.com/pod-product-compliance
Lightning Source LLC
Chambersburg PA
CBHW031438040426
42444CB00006B/870